中国当代陶艺名家

李正文作品集

主编　李哲峰

广西美术出版社

中国当代陶艺名家

李正文作品集

主编　李哲峰

责任编辑　覃西娅

封面设计　张文馨

版式设计　羿　一

责任校对　林志茂　陈小英

出版　广西美术出版社

地址　广西南宁市望园路 9 号　530022

发行　广西美术出版社发行部

电话　5701356　传真　5701355

版次　2000 年 12 月第 1 版第 1 次印刷

印刷　深圳雅昌彩色印刷有限公司

规格　1194mm × 889mm　1/16

印张　2

书号　ISBN 7-80625-839-6/J·703

印数　1000 册

定价　25 元 ／ 册

The Contemporary Famous Ceramic Artists of China

Li Zhengwen´s Works

Chief Editor ／ Li Zhefeng

Responsible Editer ／ Qin Xiya

Cover Design ／ Zhang Wenxin

Format Design ／ Yi Yi

Responsible Reviser ／ Lin Zhimao Chen Xiaoying

Published ／ Guangxi Fine Arts Publishing House

Edition time ／ The First Edition and the First Printing in December, 2000

Add ／ No.9 Wangyuan Road, Nanning, Guangxi　530022

Published ／ Published Department, Guangxi Fine Arts Publishing House

Tel ／ 5701356　　Fax ／ 5701355

Printed ／ Shenzhen Artron Color Printing CO. LTD.

Standard ／ 1194mm × 889mm　1/16

Stamp　2

Book Number ／ ISBN 7-80625-839-6/J·703

Printed Count ／ 1000

Price ／ ￥25 ／ Vol.

序

李哲峰

我似乎更愿意把现代陶艺视为当代艺术的一种，只有这样，中国现代陶艺的产生和发展才是有意义的。在我看来，中国现代陶艺的从业者首先应该是一个当代艺术家，一个致力于中国当代艺术的探索者，这才是最重要的。

陶土也许是一种特殊的媒材，人类与泥土的天然关系使之对人而言充满了亲切感。无论在西方还是东方，人类认为生的神话始终与泥土密不可分。《圣经》里说："人生于泥土，而终将归于泥土。"古代的波斯诗人也有类似的诗句，《鲁拜集》里说："那制陶的泥土，正是先人的尸骨做成。"对于中国的艺术家而言，陶土这种材料拥有明确的文化指向性，它是中国古代文明的当然代表。这种具有鲜明文化特征的媒材对于中国的当代艺术家而言，无疑具有特殊的价值和意义，也更具有挑战性。

从最初的探索开始，中国现代陶艺走过了十余年的历史。从简单地接受西方现代艺术的观念，到注重开掘传统中的现代基因，中国的艺术家们慢慢地确立了自己的风格以及前进的方向，并逐渐成熟自己。这显然是一个极其艰难的过程。出版的这套丛书，在我看来，总结了中国现代陶艺发展的十年史,代表着我们这个时代陶艺发展的高度。正是这些坚实的足迹表明中国现代陶艺的前景未可限量，充满魅力。

Preface

LI Zhefeng

I'd like to consider modern ceramic arts as one of the contemporary arts because only in this way can the birth and development of modern Chinese ceramic arts become meaningful. On the other hand, those who are engaged in modern ceramic arts in China are, first of all, contemporary artists devoting themselves to the exploration of contemporary Chinese arts.

The pottery clay can be a special medium which, as a result of the natural relationship between human beings and clays, becomes very intimate to them. Myths concerning the birth of man in both western and eastern cultures are closely related to clays. It is said in the *Bible* that man comes from the clay and will ultimately end in clay. Still there is similar saying by ancient Persian poets, *In Rubaiyat* it goes like this,"The clay used for pottery is made just of the bones of our forefathers". Clay has a definite cultural orientation for Chinese artists because it is surely a representative of the ancient Chinese civilization. Therefore, with its sharp cultural features, this medium is especially valuable and meaningful for Chinese artists, and more challenging.

Dated back to the earliest research, modern Chinese ceramic arts has witnessed a history of more than ten years. From the mere acception of the concepts of modern western arts to the attention of the exploring of modern elements in conventions, the Chinese artists have step by step established their own styles and fixed the direction of their development. They are turning more and more mature. Obviously this is an extremely hard experience. The publishing of this series is a conclusion to this ten-year stage of the development of modern Chinese ceramic arts, a summit of our age. It is these solid steps that promise an indefinite, bright future of modern Chinese ceramic arts.

淡泊·自然·雄浑

汤 麟

正文君，楚人也。以才思闻名，数十年泛舟艺海，成绩斐然，不求索取，默默奉献，有目共睹。人谓，如君者，鲜矣。诚然也。

《陶艺集》为正文君近二十年来纵情汪洋淡泊，神游自然雄浑的心物共振之作。读后深感陶艺非哲理，哲理亦非陶艺，但具有历史年轮之陶艺，却蕴涵着八方之沉思，苍穹之灵气，在泥水交融中与"圆"浑然一体。圆，为宇宙之象，无始无终。大者，混沌为圆；小者，缸瓮、钵盂、瓶罐为圆；动者，双手合抱为圆，轴车、旋盘为圆。陶艺起于"圆"，终于圆，成于圆。以圆咏叹"江上推明月"之广阔，以圆神驰"涵虚混太清"之遐想。审美上的"圆"为陶艺的灵魂，艺术上的"圆"之"轴车、旋盘"为陶艺得以灵巧的手段。凭借对"圆"与"陶"的理解，在新石器时期，我国就有了朴质的仰韶彩陶、简约的半坡壶罐、清纯的龙山黑陶、仪态逼真的牛河红陶神女。以至于伟大的先哲、艺术家、考古家、史论家都在一个大胆而深具意味的命题中，得出了共同的结论："人类的一部文化发展史是从陶艺开始"，"用火"与"制陶"是人类文化史上的第一篇章。

如果说，人类始终在追求着自我完善和最大限度的自由，陶艺是特定地区、特定民族儿童时代稚拙的创作和远古的记忆，那么，正文君陶艺所追求所体现的正是这些精神的全部含义。在创作过程中，他双手揉捏着泥土、驾御着轴车、拨动着旋盘，按照自我想象的意愿，在具抑扬顿挫的节奏中，或快或慢地控制着陶车和旋盘的速度；在随心所欲的缩束与膨胀中，给它们形体、肌肉、血液、神经和生命。为此，他痴迷到亦梦亦幻的迷狂中。他说，这就是艺术，这就是陶艺。

正文君陶艺的成就，来自对中国古典文化、道德文章、品格气质的传承和发展。他吟叹屈子的《天问》，神游老庄的混沌，面壁达摩的静思，欣赏建安的慷慨任性。他在对"撕裂"和"错位"的探索里，有闪亮的成就，也有灰色的矛盾。特别是"数字网络"和"微电脑装置"已改变我们的时空观念，在陶艺上，如何解释作为时空观念的"现代"和作为艺术观念的"现代"，这是继黑格尔后的又一艺术难题。正文君的回答是：以手工操作为主的陶艺，确实无法和智能化的"数字网络"、快速的"微电脑装置"相比，但不能忘却，它的智能、快速、灵巧，甚至它的本身都是人的创造，使用它的、掌握它的仍然是人。当陶艺家在信手揉捏泥土，双脚踏旋陶车，所得到的生理上的快感，迅速上升为心理上的美感，达到艺术畅想的境界时，这种满足，这种享受，可说是陶艺家独具的专利。有出息的陶艺家从来是对事物辩证的接受者，决不能被"人为的盲点"所蒙蔽。既以"横向的现代"扩大陶艺的视野，也以"纵向的古典"充实陶艺的灵魂。正文君的《陶艺集》有深山古潭的沉静，山狂风怒的神奇。也有"江声推月上涵虚混太清"的意境。

正文君的陶艺

汪洋淡泊

自然雄浑

是赶路者盼望的灿烂夕阳

也是赶路者盼望的曙光。

汤 麟
湖北美术学院教授、著名美学家和美术评论家，是有特殊贡献专家，享受国务院特殊津贴。

Not Seek Fame and Wealth · Natural · Vigorous and Firm

Tang Lin

Li Zhengwen is a man from Chu. With the imaginative power and creativeness is heard, several ten years sailing in the sea of arts, the achievement is striking. Not to take from, but to offer quietly, obvious to anyone who has eyes. It is said such persons are of a rarity, Really so.

"*Ceramic Arts Collection*" is the result of Zhengwen's 20 years of intoxication in the sea of simplicity and the resonance of his heart with the world after his mind's trip over the grandiose nature. Thoughts after reading: ceramic arts is no philosophic theory, and vice versa. But ceramic arts, which possesses a long history, contains thoughts of all kinds and all the subtleties under the vault of heaven. It is one integrated mass of "Sphere" blended from muddy water. A sphere is the shape of universe and it begins and ends nowhere. Speaking big, the Chaos is spherical; speaking small, bottle jars, jar urns and earthen bowls are spherical; and speaking of motion, joined hands form a circle and turning trays and axle wheels are circular. Ceramic arts begins and ends in "Sphere". Circular forms were used in the chants "the river pushing up a bright moon" to describe a vast horizontal view, and "the emptiness mingling into a sphere" to mean whimsical dreams. In beauty aesthetics, "Sphere" is the soul of ceramic arts, and the turning trays and axle wheels are the basic means for the nimble art of pottery. On the understanding of "Sphere" and "pottery", the Neo Stone Age China gave birth to the simple and unaffected Yangshao painted potteries, the terse Banpo kettle jars, the delicate Longshan black potteries and the lifelike Niuhe River red pottery goddess. So the great thinkers of the past, artists, archaeologists and historians reached the same conclusion after a bold and profound proposition:"The first chapter of human civilization began with pottery","the use of fire", and "the making of pottery" wrote the first chapter in the human cultural history.

If mankind is seeking self – improvement and the utmost freedom from the very beginning, and ceramic arts is the childhood memory of a distant and clumsy period in a particular district or nation, then what Zhengwen has been seeking in his ceramic arts is the full meaning of those spirit. In the course of ceramic making, his hands are kneading "earth", steering the axle wheels, shifting the turning trays, and giving his objects the form, muscle, blood, nerve and life, according to his imagination, with the rhyming movement of pause and transition in controlling the turning trays and axle wheels and his willful formal expansion and contraction. With it, he has been indulging himself to a dreamlike fascination. He says this is arts, ceramic arts. The achievement of Zhengwen's ceramic arts comes from his inheriting and developing the classic Chinese culture, the morals and ethics and characteristic temperaments and qualities. He chants Quzi's "*Heaven Asks*", broods over Laozhuang's Chaos, meditates Damo's meditations and appreciates the generosity and willfulness of Jianan. In his "Laceration" and "Dislocation", he has glaring achievements as well as gray contradictions. Especially the "Digital Network" and "Microcomputer Device" present, while changing our time and space concept, the problem of the "modern" concept in artistic and temporal context, one other art problem after Hagale. The answer by Zhengwen is: Ceramic arts that depends on manual operations can not be placed with the intelligent "Digital Network" or the fast "Microcomputer Device". But one should not forget these intelligent machines are made and controlled by humans. The ceramic artists have their patented pleasure and satisfaction when kneading the clays and paddling the turning trays and when the physical sensation soaring into the psychological satisfaction and drifting artistic realm. A promising ceramic artist is always an accepter of dialectic truth, never to be fooled by the "artificial blind spots". The "horizontal modernity" can expand the horizon of ceramic arts and the "vertical tradition" enrich the soul of the art. Zhengwen's *Ceramic Arts Collection* has the quietness of an ancient pool in remote mountains and the magical spell of crazy mountains and angry gales as well as the literary mood of "wave sounds pushing up the moon, the emptiness mingling into a sphere".

The Ceramic arts of Zhengwen is vast like ocean, naturally vigorous and firm, showing high ideals in simplicity.

It is the magnificent evening sun for the hurrying traveller, also the first light of morning to him.

Tang Lin, a professor of Hubei Fine Arts College, as well as a famous aesthetics scholar and fine arts critic, he enjoys the special subsidy of State Department as an expert of special contribution.

创 作 自 述

李正文

陶艺是心灵的艺术，做陶的人应该有点禅的态度，常常是过程比结果更重要。其中感性的因素相对要多一些。做陶仿佛对人有巨大的磁力，常常一接触陶就会在不知不觉中迷恋上它，以至废寝忘食，如醉如痴。

湖北曾经是中国陶瓷的重要基地：自新石器时代屈家岭的红陶、商代盘龙的原始瓷和白陶、南朝的青瓷、宋代武昌湖泗窑的影青，直到近代蕲春、麻城的刻花坛，汉川系马口的灰釉刀马人，它们"独行特立，各领风骚"。我在接触和深入学习的过程中，逐步体验到陶的人文内涵，认识传统陶瓷发展到现代陶艺的深刻背景与巨大潜力。

陶艺材质的品性弥漫着宽厚、质朴与理性的严峻，具有强烈的震撼力。现代陶艺多变的手法及巨大的魅力，是那样的不可抗拒。而具有禅性哲理的做陶过程，使人净化心性，回归自然，身心与大自然融为一体。

自幼生长于长江之滨的我，热衷表现那些活跃的生命：水乡池塘的小鱼、荷叶、莲蓬；从湛蓝的天空到阳光耀眼的湖水。这些童年生活的记忆，如今却变得那样遥远模糊而不可及，成为现实中的梦境 而面对的现实却是被污染的江河和人的异化、人与被煎熬的可怕图景。我力求在我的创作中表达我的意念、想象和希望。

在陶艺创作的全过程中，心灵会受到一次次冲击和震颤。从柔软的陶泥到坚硬如钢的成品，从曲折变化、充满动势的形体到烈焰中凝固而再生，陶艺的非制模性，最直接、真实地留下你对形体的感受和痕迹。做陶的过程充满痛苦和快乐，当看见作品一次次失败，一次次开裂、扭曲和倒塌，由不能忍受到自觉承受，这个过程是心灵和精神的升华，失败痛苦之后将是成功的巨大欢愉。

陶土的多样、釉水的神秘、火的深奥——这些不可预测的组合、偶发的因素，高深莫测，如临深渊，这是人与大自然造物主共同创造的产物。天、地、人、"四季"、"五行"（金、木、水、火、土）相生相克；成功的艰难和巨大的偶然性，使陶艺创作的全过程充满了刺激与挑战。

制陶人的路将是漫长而望不到尽头，一条长线贯穿数千年陶瓷文明，传承文明的下线连接着新世纪的发展。人们习惯称 21 世纪为数字化信息时代，当然这也应该是属于现代陶艺发展的时代。中国现代陶艺在经过痛苦的褴褛期后，必将在新的世纪展现中国陶瓷曾经拥有的雍容大度、宽厚内敛、充满普遍的人性。历史将再一次证明：无论"官仔大款、市井小民、江湖黑道，直至目不识丁的山野农夫、村姑、贩夫、走卒"，都无不被陶的魅力所征服，他们的心灵同样受到震撼和激荡，并与其生活、精神世界产生千丝万缕的联系；而相对那些被地位、财富、名利身家所累和心力交瘁的人们而言，应该说：

做陶的人是幸运的。

An Account in the Artist's Own Words

Li Zhengwen

Ceramics is the art of heart, the man that does it should have the attitude of a Buddhist, and often its course is more important than the result. There is relatively more of a perception factor and a seemingly huge magnetic force attracting the person who does it. Often One's contact with it makes one unconsciously indulge in it, forgetting eating and sleeping, as if intoxicated and stupefied.

Hubei Province was once the important base of Chinese pottery and porcelain: from the red pottery of Qu Jialing in the Neo Stone Age, the primitive porcelain and white pottery of the Shang Era, the celadon of the Southern Dynasty and the shadowy celadon made by the Wuchang Husi Kiln in the Song Dynasty up to the modern engraved floral–design jars made in Qichun and Machen and the gray glazed sabre horse man made in Ximakou of Hanchuan, they "turned over a unique chapter in leading the various styles". In the course of my practice and study, I gradually experienced and grasped the character and the deep humanity connotation of pottery, realizing the profound background and huge latent capacity of its development from the traditional pottery and porcelain to the modern ceramic arts.

The quality of ceramic material is brimmed with grace, modesty and rational austerity, and the varied methods of modern ceramic arts are so glamorous and captivating. The ceramic making process which embodies the Zen philosophy can purify human minds, making body and mind melt into an organic whole with the nature.

I was born beside Yangtse River and I have been in love with those ponds and lakes, the brisk life of small fish, lotus leaves and seedpods; and the blue sky and the dazzling water in the sunlight. Those childhood memories have now become so distant and intangible like a dreamland in reality; the reality facing us is the polluted river and the alienation of man, and the fearful view of suffering of man and nature. I make every effort to express in my works my ideas, imaginations and hopes.

In the course of ceramic arts making, I have undergone much shock and trembling in my heart. From the soft mud to the hard, finished product, the tortuous and dynamic form solidifies in the flame and is reborn. The non – mould characteristics of ceramic arts most directly and truly keeps your feelings and traces of form. It is full of pains and joys, seeing the works failed, cracked, distorted and collapsed. From feeling unbearable to the awareness of its course is a sublimation of the soul and spirit, and what will bring after is the huge happiness of success.

The varied pottery's clay, the mysterious glaze color and the abstruse fire–those unpredictable combinations and accidental factors are so unfathomable that you are like facing an abyss. This is the product of a joined creation between man and nature. Heaven, earth, man, "four seasons" and "the five elements" (gold, wood, water, fire and soil) have their mutual promotions and restraints. The difficulty and the huge contingency of success make the full course of ceramic making full of excitement and challenge.

The road for a ceramic artist is long and endless, a long thread runs through the thousand–year civilization in pottery and porcelain making with its end linking to the development of the new century. People say the 21st century is a time of digitalization and the information, it is certainly a time also for the development of modern ceramic arts. The modern ceramic arts of China, after the painful swaddling period, must resume its former grace and magnanimity in the new century. History will prove once again: whether it be "tycoons or officers, marketplace small people or outlaws, illiterate farmers or village girls, peddlers or lackeys", they will all be conquered by the glamour of pottery without exception because ceramics has countless ties with their daily lives and spiritual world. A ceramic artist will say to the people tired by position, wealth and fame : The man that does pottery is fortunate.

1. 1997年在汉口青少年宫陶艺馆创作"荷塘"系列
2. 1992年与美国陶艺家温格比在工作室合影
3. 2000年，在工作室之一
4. 在拉坯
5. 在工作室之二
6. 1988年在"香港国际陶艺研讨会及作品展"展台前与台湾评
   论家宋龙飞(方叔)合影

1	2
3	4
	5
	6

1. Produced works of the "*Lotus Series*" in Hankou Adolescent Palace Ceramic Arts Hall in 1997
2. Had a group photo with Wengeber, the American ceramis artist in the studio in 1992
3. In 2000, in the studio No.1
4. Doing earthen brick
5. In the studio No.2
6. Had a group photo with Song Longfei, the critic of Taiwan in front of the "Symposium and Works Exhibition of International Ceramic Arts in Hong Kong" in 1988

生命系列——世界
陶　1988 年
43cm × 10cm × 20cm
还原焰 1200℃

Life series, World
Pottery 1988
43cm × 10cm × 20cm
Reducing flame 1200℃

生命系列——椿
陶　1988 年
20cm × 20cm × 43cm
柴烧 1280℃

Life series, Chinese toon
Pottery 1988
20cm × 20cm × 43cm
Brushwood burning 1280℃

生命系列——始
陶　1988 年
27cm × 21cm × 25cm
氧化焰 1280℃

Life series, Beginning
Pottery 1988
27cm × 21cm × 25cm
Oxidizing flame 1280℃

轮
陶　1990年
28cm × 12cm × 39cm
氧化焰　1150℃

Wheel
Pottery 1990
28cm × 12cm × 39cm
Oxidizing flame 1150℃

渴
陶　1990 年
37cm × 37cm × 23.5cm
氧化焰　1150℃

Thirsty
Pottery 1990
37cm × 37cm × 23.5cm
Oxidizing flame 1150℃

涸
陶　1991 年
37cm × 14cm × 40cm
氧化焰　1150℃

Dry
Pottery 1991
37cm × 14cm × 40cm
Oxidizing flame 1150℃

井
陶　1991 年
27cm × 25cm × 32cm
柴烧　1280℃

Well
Pottery 1991
27cm × 25cm × 32cm
Brushwood burning 1280℃

长满青苔的井台
釉陶　1992 年
32cm × 20cm × 26cm
氧化焰　1200℃

The wellhead with lichen
Glazed pottery 1992
32cm × 20cm × 26cm
Oxidizing flame 1200℃

木椅
釉陶　1992 年
17cm × 13cm × 26cm
还原焰　1280℃

Wooden chair
Glazed pottery 1992
17cm × 13cm × 26cm
Reducing flame 1280℃

青铜联想系列——井
陶 1995 年
18cm × 10cm × 26cm
氧化焰 1180℃

The associational series of bronze, Well
Pottery 1995
18cm × 10cm × 26cm
Oxidizing flame 1180℃

青铜联想系列——蛙
釉瓷 1996 年
18cm × 9cm × 26cm
还原焰 1320℃

The associational series of bronze, Frog
Vitreous enamel 1996
18cm × 9cm × 26cm
Reducing flame 1320℃

青铜联想系列——波
釉瓷 1998
17cm × 10cm × 15cm
还原焰 1320℃

The associational series of bronze, Wave
Vitreous enamel 1998
17cm × 10cm × 15cm
Reducing flame 1320℃

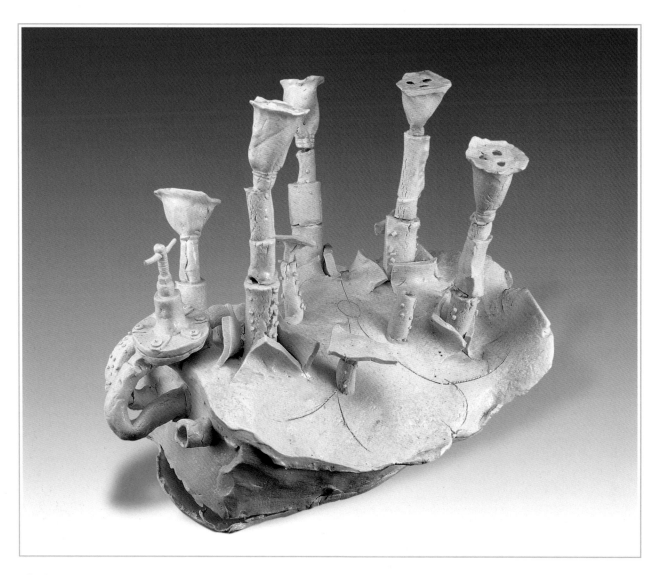

荷塘系列——伸
釉瓷　1994 年
30cm × 23cm × 30cm
还原焰　1350℃

Lotus series, Extened
Vitreous enamel 1994
30cm × 23cm × 30cm
Reducing flame 1350℃

青铜联想系列——缚
釉瓷　1999 年
17cm × 10cm × 15cm
还原焰　1320℃

The associational series of bronze, String
Vitreous enamel 1999
17cm × 10cm × 15cm
Reducing flame 1320℃

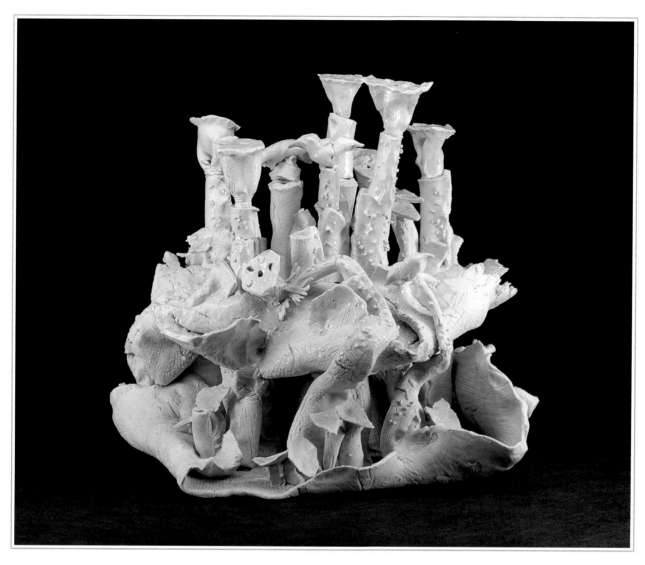

荷塘系列——夏
釉瓷 1996 年
38cm × 32cm × 32cm
还原焰 1350℃

Lotus series,Summer
Vitreous enamel 1996
38cm × 32cm × 32cm
Reducing flame 1350℃

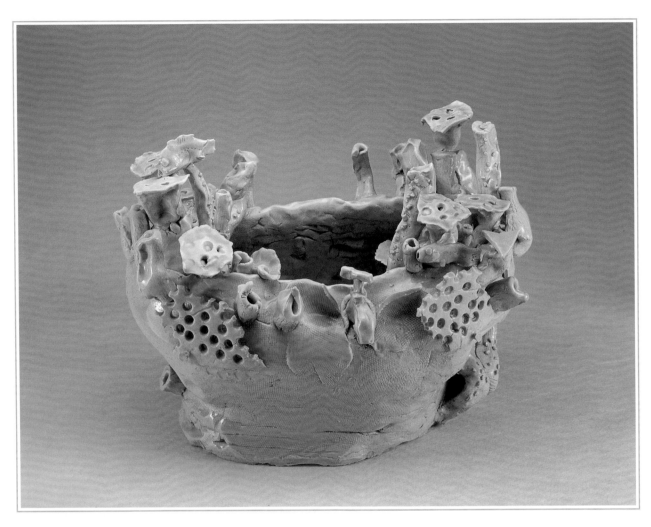

荷塘系列——盆栽
釉瓷　1997 年
33cm × 23cm × 25cm
氧化焰 1350℃

Lotus series,Potted plant
Vitreous enamel 1997
33cm × 23cm × 25cm
Oxidizing flame 1350℃

荷塘系列——迎风
釉瓷　1997 年
30cm × 17cm × 21cm
还原焰　1350℃

Lotus series,Windward
Vitreous enamel 1997
30cm × 17cm × 21cm
Reducing flame 1350℃

荷塘系列——霜冻
釉瓷　1998 年
36cm × 26cm × 19cm
还原焰　1280℃

Lotus series,Frost
Vitreous enamel 1998
36cm × 26cm × 19cm
Reducing flame 1280℃

荷塘系列——风
釉瓷 1998 年
39cm × 14cm × 50cm
还原焰 1280℃

Lotus series,Wind
Vitreous enamel 1998
39cm × 14cm × 50cm
Reducing flame 1280℃

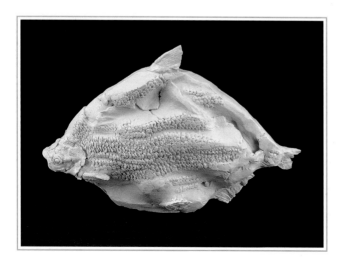

武昌鱼
瓷 1996 年
43cm × 9cm × 28cm
还原焰 1350℃

Wuchang fish
Porcelain 1996
43cm × 9cm × 28cm
Reducing flame 1350℃

绳·结
釉陶　1996 年
27cm × 10cm × 39cm
氧化焰　1280℃

Rope, Knot
Glazed pottery 1996
27cm × 10cm × 39cm
Oxidizing flame 1280℃

绳·结·圈
釉瓷　1998 年
37cm × 17cm × 40cm
还原焰　1280℃

Rope, Knot, Circle
Vitreous enamel 1998
37cm × 17cm × 40cm
Reducing flame 1280℃

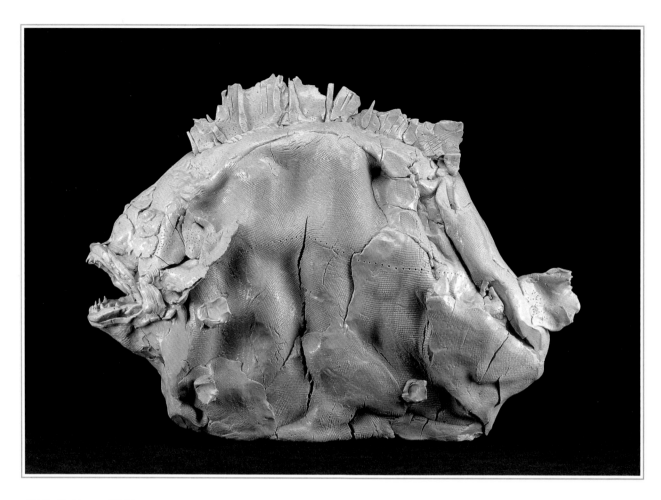

鳜鱼系列——潜游
釉瓷　1997 年
47cm × 17cm × 34cm
还原焰　1350℃

Mandarin fish,Diving swim
Vitreous enamel 1997
47cm × 17cm × 34cm
Reducing flame 1350℃

鳜鱼系列——自游
釉瓷　1998 年
50cm × 20cm × 40cm
还原焰　1350℃

Mandarin fish,Swim alone
Vitreous enamel 1998
50cm × 20cm × 40cm
Reducing flame 1350℃

鳜鱼系列——污染
釉瓷　1998 年
40cm × 12cm × 30cm
还原焰　1300℃

Mandarin fish, Pollute
Vitreous enamel 1998
40cm × 12cm × 30cm
Reducing flame 1300℃

混沌
陶　1998 年
31cm × 12cm × 14cm
还原焰　1280℃

Chaos
Pottery 1998
31cm × 12cm × 14cm
Reducing flame 1280℃

世纪之交
釉瓷　1999 年
28cm × 12cm × 43cm
还原焰　1280℃

The join of century
Vitreous enamel 1999
28cm × 12cm × 43cm
Reducing flame 1280℃

架与影——残
陶　1999 年
35cm × 11cm × 27cm
氧化焰　1200℃

Frame and shadow,Incomplete
Pottery 1999
35cm × 11cm × 27cm
Oxidizing flame 1200℃

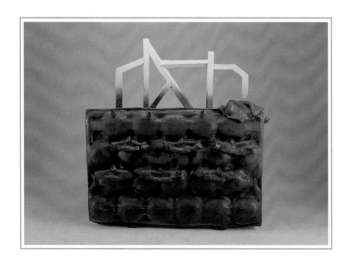

架与影——泄
陶　2000 年
47cm × 17cm × 46cm
氧化焰　1230℃

Frame and shadow, Discharge
Pottery 2000
Size 47cm × 17cm × 46cm
Oxidizing flame 1230℃

架与影——崩
陶 1999 年
50cm × 31cm × 35cm
氧化焰 1200℃

Frame and shadow,Collapse
Pottery 1999
50cm × 31cm × 35cm
Oxidizing flame 1200℃

葫芦
陶 2000 年
12cm × 12cm × 23cm
氧化焰 1100℃

Gourd
Pottery 2000
12cm × 12cm × 23cm
Oxidizing flame 1100℃

展
瓷 2000 年
13cm × 13cm × 30cm
还原焰 1300℃

Stretch
Porcelain 2000
13cm × 13cm × 30cm
Reducing flame 1300℃

艺术年表

个展

| 1992 年 | 李正文陶艺雕塑展 | 中国·台湾 |

参展

1981 年	首届全国城雕展	中国·湖北
1985 年	首届全国陶艺家邀请展	中国·湖北
1988 年	中国传统陶艺及现代陶艺作品展	中国·香港
1990 年	湖北省首届现代陶艺大展	中国·湖北
1991 年	北京'91 国际陶艺研讨会年展	中国·北京
1995 年	景德镇国际陶艺邀请展	中国·景德镇
1996 年	陶瓷的国度——中国当代陶艺巡回展	欧洲
1998 年	日中陶艺交流展	中国·湖北
1999 年	中日陶艺交流展	日本·东京

获奖

| 1985 年 | 获轻工业部"中国工艺美术百花奖"创作设计 | 一等奖 |

其他

1981 年	在《美术》杂志上发表"葛洲坝四面体大江截流纪念碑"作品方案	
1988 年	在"中国传统陶艺及现代陶艺研讨会"上发表论文 《陶艺与禅境——直观、创造、生命》	中国·香港
1993 年	在《艺术家》杂志上发表作品《涸》、《渴》、《火神——祝融》	中国·台湾
1997 年	在《美术文献》上发表"荷塘系列"作品	

ARTISTIC CHRONOLOGY

Solo Exhibitions

1992　Li Zhengwen's Personal Ceramic and Sculpture Art Exhibition Taiwan, China

Group Exhibitions

1981　The First Urban Sculpture Exhibition in Hubei, China

1985　The First Session of Chinese Ceramic Artists Invitation Show in Hubei, China.

1988　The Exhibition of Modern and Traditional Ceramic Arts of China in H.K., China

1990　The First Hubei Province Modern Ceramic Arts Exhibition in Hubei, China

1991　The '91 Beijing International Ceramic Arts Symposiums and Exhibition in Beijing, China

1995　The Jingdezhen International Ceramic Arts Invitation Show in Jingdezhen, China

1996　Ceramic State-the Touring Exhibition of Contemporary Chinese Ceramic Arts in Europe

1998　The Sino-Japanese Ceramics Exchange Exhibition in Hubei, China

1999　The Sino-Japanese Ceramics Exchange Exhibition in Tokyo, Japan

Prizes

1985　Won the "First Design Prize of Chinese Arts and Crafts" issued by the Light Industry Ministry of China

Others

1981　Making the scheme for "Tetrahedron Monument for Gezhou Dam" which was published in "*Fine Arts Magazine*"

1988　Publishing the thesis "*Ceramic Arts and Zen-Intuition, Greativity and Life*" in the "Symposium of Modern and Traditional Ceramic Arts of China" in H.K., China

1933　"*Artist*" magazine Published the works "*Drying*", "*Yearning*" and "*God of Fire*" in Taiwan, China

1997　"*Fine Arts Documents*" Published the works "*Lotus Series*"